Powerful Healing

Rachel Milligan

BookLeaf
Publishing

India | USA | UK

Presentation by *BookLeaf Publishing*

Web: www.bookleafpub.com

E-mail: info@bookleafpub.com

ISBN: 9789363304406

First edition 2024

I want to thank Lauren Brill for coming up with "The Unsealed", the community that inspired my love for writing and my love for poems. It gave me the inspiration to do this challenge and to evolve and grow. Grow into the person that I'm meant to be.

The Burning Fire of Words

Dear Lauren Brill,
Struggles upon struggles
Fighting to find hope in the madness
Wishing for the speed of airplanes
Then I found a connection
To something powerful
To something much more meaningful
To the countless time writing
Writing these poems
The blazing, exploding sun
Getting everything blown up to bits
Messages being erased
Hopefully to inspire and spread awareness
To the problems and love to this world

One Step Further

Broken bones
Afraid to let go
But remember
The old school communication
The frequent letters
The box of chocolates
The continuing thought process
The same song stuck in your head
The darkness that rolled over you
Disrupting the happiness
The constant sorrows
The irrational thoughts
Scrolling through the memories
Burning you like flames
To where you are no more
Becoming the ash
Doesn't consume you as much anymore
With the cords slowly untying
The guitar becomes in tune
The Legos being built
The staircases that hardly tumble

Racing Sunset

So beautiful and so bright
Blink and you'll miss it
Soon darkness will take over
Not enough time to see everything
But knowing there will be more
More beautiful people
More beautiful inspirations
More beautiful thoughts
Don't let it consume you
Move on to the next
Move on to the never-ending person
Don't let one person take that away from you
Take away everything you've worked so hard for
Take away what makes you smile like the
sunrise
Take away the mountains you have built
The staircases you have climbed
The sun that you see in the morning
The way you take in the moment of peace
The way you get excited
And the joy you get from living

Fly me to the Clouds

Dear you,
Look up,
Look up at the clouds of the sky,
The pouring of rain in another part of town
The demons yesterday don't come to scare you
in the dark today
It is giving a better future
Maybe that's what was meant to happen
It gives you more muscle
To run a marathon
More determination to keep on going
Sometimes flowers need to die before they can
fully grow
I know its hard
Wishing you were doing great
But to become stronger
You have to let the birds migrate
Not to stay stuck in quicksand
To become a better version of yourself
Let the horses roam
Heal today
Don't create movies of darkness
Grow enough to the point of loving yourself
where people don't affect you

You will be okay

Think back to all the things you thought you did
wrong
The always leaving town for somewhere new
Needing to take a breath
Feeling the sense people hated me
Feeling the pressure to be perfect
To be the same as everyone else
Swimming in a lake full of tears
Trying to say the right things
Become the right person
Being so consumed by people's lives
Not worrying about your own
Remember to give yourself grace
For that point in time
Don't worry about people's thoughts, people's
movements, and people's lives
Don't worry about being too much, or being a
bother to the one who you thought mattered
most
The constant stress, the constant love and worry
about that person
You put it out there
And all you can do is breathe,
Some things were meant to happen for a better
tomorrow

Too far deep in the ocean
But that's all okay
You will be okay

Jokes flying off the wall

Sadness swirling like a tornado
Other people's amazing perspective
Different lives
Different emotions
Different forms of laughter
Colors of the building
Trying to be funny
Coping with panic rooms
The acting like a different character
Fell to the love because of you
The inspiration
The wanting to do better
Putting myself down
Underestimating myself
The constant talk about you
Not knowing what you're going to say
But trying to get other people to smile, to laugh
Laughing with some
Maybe it's not funny
But way for me to cope
Not focusing on the car crash
Sugarcoating the pain

Cords Electrifying

Hit by lightning
Worried about the future
Worried about the constant tying of the brain
Worried about not doing the math problem right
Worried about the black and white
Am I doing enough to break through to the ice
right below me
Worried about falling to the depths of the ocean
Down to the darkest part where there is nobody
around
Starting is the hard part whereas ending makes it
worth it
You will be skilled like the professionals
You will be awarded for your work
You will be proud of what you accomplish
You will be loved by many
Appreciated by lots
And most of all happy
You may be stressed, but it will be worth your
time

Can't stop thinking about you

Thought I was healed
But then I thought about you
Got reminded of the things you do
Of the things around me
The abstract of the building
All the people that come with that
The 3 full of stories
The out-of-tune instruments
The vintage pictures playing vividly in my mind
The charm bracelets chiming in the wind
The inspirational quotes begging for attention
The messages that won't stop burning
The made-up scenarios haunting me with ghosts
The hope you'll notice the rich hotels beaming
with life
The importance of the things that matter most to
me
The acting world burning to ash
Makes me think of you

Mouth Zipped Shut

Love talking to you
Like a speed rush
Of a brain freeze
Don't dive deep
Deeper to the root of the volcano
Be careful what you say
May not like the answer of the play
Ears that might push it away
Shielding the painful
Like a dream catcher fighting against the wind
Don't let the uncomfortable fear tear you down
Like ripping sheets of paper into ash
Burning everything to shreds
Don't want to deal with the consequences
Better belt up
Fight the unknown
Would I be full of regrets like a box full of
secrets
Or will I be hurt from not saying it
Saying what I want
or not saying what I don't want
Worse impulsively saying something
Get out of my brain into the very depths of the
mind
Into the place where I am brain dead

Where I don't remember a single thought
Where they are buried deep into the ground
The place where there is no more
Throwing away the thoughts into a black hole
Where nothing remains
Or to the depths of hell burning it to death

Endless Screaming

Screaming till the earth bleeds
Till your brain explodes and there is no more
Till the lying gets zipped shut.
Breaking bones making the earth shatter
Creating a new earth
A new brain
Baking from scratch
To whats true
Whereas assumptions breaks a window
Going far into the depths of hell
To another planet
Far far away
Years to get there
Or you will be dead
Listening to the lions roar
faintly in the distance
Where consciousness breaks

Darkness

Take me to the grave
Where the skeletons roam
Where the wind blows aganist the ground
Where the trees stand still
Take me to the place where I feel most alone
To the place where there are crickets
Take me to the pet semetary
To the scarecrows that haunt the night
Take me to the place where bees sting
To the place where trees are burned to the
ground
Where your burned to ashes
Take me to the place where it hurts most
To the place I don't want to be anymore
To the place where you can't breathe
To the place where demons haunt you
Let me be free

Dear brain

To the thoughts that are open
Go back to space where you deserve to go
Work out so hard attachments go away
Remember who you've been
Remember the lights that flicker will work again
Go through them
Go through the pain till there is no more
Find the climbing gym
Make the impossible possible
Go through the black to get to the other side
Don't get flatter everyday
Get in the car and move
Race your car as fast as it will go
Turn slightly
Don't spin out of control
Don't let them win
Don't let them win the race
Don't let the hackers hack your brain
Fly on your own path
Fly through the clouds
Remember all that you have
Bring the pieces together
To the ones that fit
To create a beautiful picture
Where the birds sing

Where the water flows
Where it brings you peace

Growing up

Simple things
Little houses
Posters on the walls
Recapture the good ol times
The friendship bracelet's burning bright
The Wii games playing hard
The late night movies playing in the background
Talking until you lose your voice
Mom's phone ringing in the distance
Drama seeking fast
Problems surging just above the water
Have to solve them before its too late
Trying to break habits you've done for years
The doing things on your own
School building on what you want to do
Long hours fighting you
Praying for peace
Praying to be something
Praying to be worthwhile

Be kind to the mind

Brain development for the soul
Curious to how we work and operate
To the way we are
To the different ways we think
To why we act the way we do
Too many thoughts
Too many emotions
Take care of your only brain
Involves your mental health
Involves thinking positively
Involves reframing your thoughts
Go through the ocean waves
Go through a light bulb
Till you light the city on fire
Take control of what you were given
Till the world lights up
Till the fireflies lose their glow
Fight your inner meaning
The meaning that brings you life.
The leaves that won't stop turning
The inner workings of human beings
Just trying their best to survive
Continue till the earth stops
Keep living till the sun blows up
Live as long as you can

Dream till you can't no more
Inspire till you can't breathe
Take care of yourself
Till you can't anymore

I want you

I want to talk to you
about anything and everything
I want to shout from the rooftops
I want to pull you aside
I want to see you here
I want to love you with all my might
I want to spin you around the earth
Dance till we're out of breath
Have fun till the world explodes
The regret for not taking you sooner
I want to feel the breeze aganist our necks
I want to wrap you around as many blankets as it
takes to keep you warm
Breathe till your breath turns to frost
Frost like not being able to walk
Being so frozen your mouth drops
Where the lights won't stop flickering
Where everything turns to ice
Frozen in time
Where the ghosts will not haunt you
Where nobody is moving except me and you
Like where magnets attract
A force so huge
Like light sabers in the sky

Like Poseidon's trident crushing everything that
comes between us
Blood boiling hot
Heart rate exceeding the limit
Going faster than the speed limit
While we are moving slow
Like a sloth moving up a tree
Looking straight forward at the window
Treating each other like gods
Living in our own form of heaven
With golden walls
The straight and intricate lines of the building
In Spain or in Italy
The holiness of the church
A safe place for us
A place where we can be in peace
House like in Twilight
With the glass windows
In the middle of nowhere looking in
Where no one can find us
Where we watch the deer roam
The sunshine that breaks through
The phones reflections shining
Where the flowers breeze by
Like dandelions that blow in the wind
And the joy of the party blow whistles

Pile of Worms

Trying to distract
With the games you play
With the moves you choose
With the endless laughter
With doing things that you know bring you joy
Diamonds blinding you
Fighting the urge to be reminded by you
Fighting the memories we used to have
Fighting all the talks
Fighting the staring at you
Fighting the hoping could talk to you
But lets be real here.
The wanting to go home
The thinking of you while watching a movie
Hoping you would be proud of me
Taking steps backward
Back to not having fun
Trying to push her away
Away to where the tornado sucks it in
Swirling till there's nothing left
Trying to fill the void
Losing sight of life
The happiness getting away from you
Leaving your soul
Houses crashing down

Covered in gasoline
Letting the poison swallow you whole
Losing sight fast
Trying to control it till you become blind
Anything fun turns into a asylum
Turning into the person you don't want to be
Turning your insides inside out
To a pile
To a pile of worms investing your brain
Killing you from top to bottom
disintegrating everything to dust

Dear Molly

Light up the room like stars
Floating in all directions
Building connections to the nicest people
The questions that never go un answered
The moments of advice that go far
The relatedness of it all
The love when I get to see you
The cheering you on every chance I get
To the incredible person you are
To all the helping hands
Leading me to the place I'm meant to be
Where wildflowers grow
Where trophies exist

Waiting

Patience is key
That's what they all say
Patience can either help you or hurt you
Help you to find the things that bring you peace
Help you to find who you're meant to be
Closer to loving yourself
Closer to not letting people bring you down
Closer to being successful
Closer to finding your group of people
Or patience can be hurtful
Hurtful in constantly waiting
Waiting for something to happen
Waiting for that supernova to hit ground zero
going through the motions everyday
Not really living
Instead of congratulating the journey
Counting the steps
The steps to the top
Losing your soul to darkness
Losing your own worth
Remember to not spend your time waiting
Don't thin about waiting
Be present where you are
Be grateful where you are now
Growing is a never-ending process

You will never stop growing
Be satisfied to what your life is
What's it looking like
As long as you keep on that trek
Don't let anything stop you
You have the power to change your life
You have the power to turn to a different channel
To change the way you look at things
To change to a different planet
Changing the colors of the stars
Keeping them in the sky
Keeping them from exploding
Destroying everything it touches

Different Worlds

I feel it in my bones
In God's realm
Surrounded by gold
With angles swarming
Which would cost a fortune on earth
That's where I come from
I'm just a girl living
Living because of you
You come from the inside of a butterfly
From deep in the wings
From something words can't explain
Where fairies exist
The most beautiful existence
You are multiple flowers in a flower field
The scenery in British Columbia
To the tall mountains
With the lakes below
Where the water is the most clear
Staring at the bow
You being the gold
I am stuck in your world
I am a prisoner stuck with chains
Screaming where silence comes out of my
mouth
I exist in prison without people hearing me

Attacking me over constant hours
Burning over and over again
I scream stop but everyday just stares like I'm
nothing to them
Glass pokes my eyes every time I think of
escaping
Scraping away everything I care about
I am in another country
Where there is nothing
No sky just black
Black as far as you can see
I am in flashing lights
Flashing lights to make me go insane
When the migraines won't stop
Music so loud all you can hear is thump, thump
Till the point you can't think
Hurting you if you ever decide to leave

Scream like a lion

Look around,
Surrounded by people
This means you are not the only one
You're a flower blooming slowly
Nobody is picture-perfect
In perfect frames
Your a number of chords
You may be a little bit out of tune
But can retune oneself
Remember to stop and breathe
You have full control
You can refocus your mind
Stop otherworldly distractions
You can heal your soul
Be free like a dandelion
Scream like a lion
Facing your doubts and fears
Proud of the progress
Proud of the road
Look at the stars
Beautiful and bright
Going with the ocean waves

Yellow Brick Road

You are who you are
Only uniquely you
Lucky to be you
Don't chase the bears
Don't apologize for the things you do
For the paths you choose
You're not the animal of the show
Not the mirror where everybody is looking
Focused on themselves
Focused on their own lives
Focused on the school work
Focused on closer relationships
Soon it will all be gone
Soon summer will hit
Soon you will wear the robes
Be out in the world
Be successful
Doing great things
And learning and growing
Into the person I'm meant to be
All good and all well